HOUSE WITH THE MANSARD ROOF

Frances Sackett's poetry has been published in numerous journals and anthologies and she has two previous collections of poetry: *The Hand Glass* (Seren) and *Cradle of Bones* (The High Window Press). Born in Wales, landscape often inspires her poetry. Her poems speak of Love, Loss, War, and how history can be revealed – maybe centuries later – through archaeological finds.

Frances is a prize-winning poet with poems placed in the Cardiff International Competition, Cheshire Prize for Literature Anthologies and The Pre-Raphaelite Society Poetry Competition. Now retired, she previously worked in a bank, a bookshop, and as a tutor for Manchester University's 'Courses for the Public'.

House with the Mansard Roof

Frances Sackett

Valley Press

First published in 2022 by Valley Press
Woodend, The Crescent, Scarborough, YO11 2PW
www.valleypressuk.com

ISBN 978-1-912436-80-4
Cat. no. VP0197

Copyright © Frances Sackett 2022

The right of Frances Sackett to be identified as the
author of this work has been asserted in accordance with
the Copyright, Designs and Patents Act 1988.

All rights reserved. No part of this publication may be
reproduced, stored in or introduced into a retrieval system,
or transmitted in any form, by any means (electronic,
mechanical, photocopying, recording or otherwise) without
prior written permission from the rights holders.

A CIP record for this book is available from the British Library.

Cover and text design by Peter Barnfather.
Edited by Jo Brandon.

Cover artwork by Edward Hopper (American, 1882–1967).
The Mansard Roof, 1923. Watercolour over graphite on paper, 13 ⅞ × 20 in.
Brooklyn Museum, Museum Collection Fund, 23.100.
© Heirs of Josephine Hopper.
Licensed by Artists Rights Society (ARS) NY/DACS, London 2022.

Printed and bound in Great Britain by
Imprint Digital, Upton Pyne, Exeter.

Contents

Arno 11

House with the Mansard Roof 12

The Suburbs 14

The Yde Girl 15

The Bones Dreaming 17

Ship Burial 18

Dead Trees 19

Skyline – M56 – Sunset 20

Moon in Flood 21

Waterfall 22

The Stillness of Country Stations 23

Childhood Illnesses 24

Damsons 25

Moths in the Agapanthus 26

In the Footsteps of Bashō 27

Albanian Spring 28

Former Person, Former Place 29

Birthright 31

Iron Shoes on the Embankment 32

Henryk Górecki at Auschwitz   33

Letters to Malta   34

Winter Coats   41

The Open Window   42

Memory   43

Eve   44

Penelope   46

Bride   47

Fossil   48

Flood   49

Inheritance   50

The Brink   51

Giverny   52

Heron   53

Bare trees   54

Drowned   55

Laptop Lover   56

Guidelines for Illuminators   57

This is Just to Say…   58

Falling for Milton 59

The Taxidermist 60

Escape Artist 61

Disappearing Men 62

Luggage 63

Desert Ghosts 64

Boy Singer 65

Over the Border 66

The Asphalt Road 68

That Afternoon 69

Sweet Idleness 70

Nude in Movement 71

Vincent 72

'Window of Vincent's Studio at the Asylum, 1889' 74

Moon Walk – July 1969 75

Acknowledgements 77

Notes on the poems 78

for Dawn & Vikki

Arno

At dusk, bats aim at your head
and the Arno is lit with darting
manoeuvres, purple hills darken
as Florence yields to the dying heat.

In a breeze that lifts off the river
old love stories fold around you.
The cobbles roll under your feet
and you almost see Dante turn
at the corner of the *Ponte Vecchio*.

Above the river a window hangs
where a girl looks across to the *Duomo*.
She has found love in this city among
its pigeons, music, art and the swift
anger to death of Latin resentment.

We walk here as the river turns amber.
Lights drop into the water in golden chains.
Near the *Uffizi* a gypsy quartet begins playing,
their music breaks on the taut eroticism
simmering in every stone.

House with the Mansard Roof

after Edward Hopper

In the stillness of a Sunday morning
you are the only inhabitant
in a world of rising heat.

If you entered any door you would find
yourself and a dream of yourself
mingle with the interior dust.

At the railroad, signal-box windows
light up with the amber-green of sunset,
tracks are silver steel
that you can treacherously cross,
but take you nowhere.

In the house with the mansard roof
there is only isolation. Trees cast
shadows against the white balconies
like the dark graphics of charcoal,
awnings billow as a storm rocks the shutters,
gables and chimney-stacks rise
in a steep confusion and attic windows
stare up at the moon.

You are a girl in a lonely city
pushing up a sash window
at the end of another day.
Your bare feet carry shadows
that follow you across the wooden floor.

The storm has brought branches down,
and trees drip with cool wetness.
You lay your arms on the window frame,
smoke another cigarette.

The Suburbs

Between each impulse
of switching on and off the lights
he would regard the way
furniture delved deeper into the walls,
the way the lithograph of a nude
shielded her nakedness behind glass
and only the moonlight throbbed
in the curtain folds.

The garden startled him
as he watched leaf shadows
dance on the bole of a tree.
He switched on the outer light –
floodlit the garden, until the sycamore
wound a long arm to impossible
heights in the sky:
silvery – luminous – silently manic.

He hid in the corner to watch,
wanting to flick on a switch,
make the dark room cosy,
the garden blind. But the room
had beckoned the moon,
its procession of ghosts,
that slipped endlessly in through the glass;
lined up on the parquet floor.

The Yde Girl

The peat cutters stepped back, spooked,
covered up their find with turves,
but re-lived the spade's slice
into the leathery sack of skull.

Then villagers came,
their archaeology indiscriminate,
they took teeth, bones,
pulled out her remaining hair.

When connoisseur robbers arrived,
they pieced the jigsaw with intricate care –
dated her to the first century –
young and small, with slight scoliosis.

The artists who reconstructed her
had trouble getting her right –
so much damage to neck and skull,
no nose to speak of.

Their waxwork metamorphosis
haunts them with a face too human –
eyes startled by the light.

Today, you might look up from your newspaper,
on the 8:40 into Amsterdam, see her
sitting opposite you – the Yde girl –

blonde hair touching her shoulders, high forehead,
clear blue eyes, and the mark on her neck
where the garrotte's knot had sunk,
on a second look, is only a mole or a lovebite.

The Bones Dreaming

The marsh sucked us in.
We sank closer, into each other's arms.
Silence now in lips and minds
and only the bones dreaming.

Above, dragonflies, marshland grasses sway;
brackish water stains our skin.
We gaze on each other,
watch time sift flesh away.

No nerves in fingertips responding,
no tingling down the spine,
only bones entwining.

And like the tributaries above us
crossing Valdaro's plain,
a tangle of bones remain
to manacle our love in death.

Ship Burial

after Sutton Hoo

Standing under the same sky
where the ship went down,
among the archaeological mounds,
what occupies this space
other than a ladybird creeping
over a child's arm, vivid sunlight,
as though gold leaf flew again
from the opened tomb?

The keeners have gone.
Even the bones have gone.
Only those worldly treasures
excavated and museumed remain.
Yet, as the enigma of a lost king is raised,
how the skeleton dissolved,
it's the ladybird found on his pillow,
gold leaf blowing like sunlight,
that rise from the wreck.

Dead Trees

You spot them as you drive through English counties,
ghostly survivors of nature's accidents.

Sometimes solitary in a field
they attract you with their *danse macabre*.

In driftwood colours, fake arms
point long witches' fingers.

Some are lightning-struck; headless skeletons,
blackened through their core.

Reminders how our dead are always there,
inhabiting the memory of a place.

Like Doggerland was once discovered
off the Norfolk coast,

and violent storms revealed
a Bronze Age forest above a beach in Wales;

ancient trees lie petrified, dreaming
of the time they lost their footing,

slipped beneath the waves.

Skyline – M56 – Sunset

Something about the wind turbines
against this fiery sunset,
the glitter of Stanlow,
the start of autumn colour,
makes you think they rule the world.

Their arms like dictators, pointing
into the sun, as though they
could pick up the fire-ball,
spin it like a Catherine wheel.

Even those ancient warriors –
pylons with hefty shoulders
seem pushed to the sidelines,
above gantries warning congestion.

And as we crawl north,
down tubes of motorway,
glimpses in the rear-view mirror
of a chemical city,
dazzling as a Manhattan skyline.

Moon in Flood

She is a hoarder of moons,
they draw her to themselves,
always different –
spare yet spacious.
For nights now the moon
has been so swollen
it seems it has burst its banks;
it wobbles low in the branches of the oak;
calls her from her bed,
where across the street
its reflection surprises her.
And in the oblivion of night hours
she sleepwalks to the back of the house,
and there it is again,
undiminished,
holding its place,
opening up a whole world,
with only the glass of the window
stopping her dropping into its arms.

Waterfall

The second I break
from the womb of this rock
the sun is on my back.
Its energy equal
to the force that
made me fall.
Each singing strand
tense to find its lute –
boundaries it dare
not push beyond.
The sparks that fly
are liquid fire.
The landscape will not burn,
I let it drink its fill.
I eat up snow,
it flowers me whiter than itself,
and in the glow of sunset
I mirror hell.
Decision is the game I play –
to follow on the given trail
or carve a newer tributary.
I'll swell this lazy river
for a while, it has a
sluggish heart. When it
has heard my native tales,
I might coerce it to division.

The Stillness of Country Stations

Victorian wrought iron and old painted benches
face the wild garden across a single line.
Willow-herb, Himalayan balsam, consort with sapling trees
as nature runs riot in the undergrowth.
It could be Adlestrop, you think.
You listen to the silence –
a chance to hear a blackbird sing.
It makes you think that England hasn't changed that much
before the train comes rattling in.

Another station – a man alights who
could have stepped from a Lowry painting –
flat cap and corded jacket,
you think you must be dreaming;
slipped back into another time,
but speed is picking up,
the train is pitching into cityscapes,
tracks are widening,
phones are singing,
and when you reach the city streets
that ghost of English countryside
dispels like ether in the cosmopolitan air.

Childhood Illnesses

They always came in summer
as though heat lay dormant beneath the skin
then finally erupted in red bursts,
blotches, itchy spots and weeping blisters.

You lay in bed listening to summer
happening outside. Smelt the breeze
weaving in through the open back door
but never quite reaching your room,

closed off as it was to keep you
isolated, lonely, with hours of
nothingness, except the strangeness
of your limp body, weak limbs.

You could faintly smell laburnum,
hear a distant tennis ball beating
rhythmically on the court;
shouts that could only be discerned

as patterns bouncing in the hot air;
domestic sounds of your mother
busy with housework you normally turned
your back on, as you headed off to school.

This was a world in another time-scale
when hours were full of imagery, sound,
sensory existence, and your heartbeat
lifting the thin sheet over you.

Damsons

They were the sweetest theft –
dark globes hanging from branches,
reaching from branches that bowed
and dandled over the hedge.

We would clamber up the ditch
and pluck their small coldness,
their silk-stone hardness.

When we bit into them, bitterness
stayed long on the tongue, drying
the mouth's juices, leaving tiny scrolls
of skin that we were reluctant to spit away.

The hoard in our pockets was what counted –
we could transport them somewhere,
lay them out, rub their bloom to dark amethyst,
then watch them mist and mottle again.

Our excuse for the theft
was the disused garden –
a wildness of forgetting and remembering.

Each year something made us return;
compelled us to that bitter fruit –
that sweet prohibition.

Moths in the Agapanthus

Something shudders beneath the flower heads.
It is past dusk, almost dark
and I think it's late for bees.

Then I see the splayed wings,
watch as they favour the underside
of these huge, blue blooms,

draw long sips of nectar, until
inebriated they sway away
like puffs of smoke.

Static, their velvet, powdery wings
display a deeper curlicue, and lost
within the agapanthus harem

they drink their fill, weave
between the long blue funnels
as though in Pompeii's street of harlots.

These peacocks of the night come unannounced,
their un-regarded work may only seem
like filaments of shifting atmosphere.

In the Footsteps of Bashō

His journey took him to a far-away land –
following the road to the deep North.
He began in Spring like the ancient poet
when Japan was aflame with cherry blossom,
the snow of Mount Fuji a distant shadow.

In his head he carried the children's words:
It took my shoes. I loved those shoes.
It swallowed the trees in front of our school.

He spoke to fishermen who had lost their livelihoods,
the old one who battled the tsunami to save his boat.
At Fukushima he wore protective clothing;
stepped out for moments in a derelict wasteland.

These were the provinces Bashō travelled,
finding the places of great importance –
the narrow road to the deep North –
arduous, beautiful, recovering slowly.

Albanian Spring

And like Persephone they have all gone into the dark –
the women whose lexicon does not admit 'rape'.

If they speak of it at all, they have been 'touched'.
And that is a word that will make them outcasts.

In the eyes of their culture they have become scum.
If their bellies grow, it's with *enemy scum*.

No lying near the heart will make their babies loved;
a consignment of hatred kicks inside them.

And from the bloody frontier of their wombs
life will spring –

like the first frail snowdrops,
abandoned to the harshest season.

Former Person, Former Place

It became too hard to study
Beowulf and Chaucer
when my country was being blown to bits.

I would sleep all day
in these rain-drenched streets
to dream of home.

Now I sell *La Perla* –
silk lingerie and cashmere jumpers,
to Italian and Japanese tourists.

London has provided us
with our ghettos –
our coffee shops and food stores.

I was half my mother
half my father,
a natural enough mix,

except the blood of Jew and Serb
together. Patterns of memory
rise up to my throat, live

in the eyes of my people
like a language of displacement.
We taste the same blood

on our tongues,
smell the Adriatic in our nostrils,
see the pale violet mountains far away.

And the beautiful word
that repeats in our ears –
Yugoslavia – Yugoslavia –

people say was a former place;
doesn't exist any more
on the map.

Birthright

They dance in the rain
they dance as bombs fall

the black glove points in the sky
they dance.

Buildings crash and fall
they take up the tune,
they dance.

Roots rise
in shifting earth,
a fork of lightning
splits the moon

they press the earth with dance.

When the wounds heal
their footprints will spoor the boundaries,
rhythm will be bedded in the land:

the land *is* dance.

Iron Shoes on the Embankment

The smallest ones, hardly more than cobbles
kicked from the embankment's paved stone,
until, up close, you see the tiny instep.

Others, slipped off, as though to enter a bath,
coupled in ownership, moulded to imperfections,
facing the cold, racing Danube.

A night in January when they dropped out
of their clothes, lastly their shoes, before
militiamen shot them into the water;

blood oozing through holes in their sides, their heads,
the river rolling them in as arms flailed
the surface and the current dragged them down.

And when you turn away – turn to cross
the bridge – they stay in your head,
breaking your heart in their simplicity,

an art form so domestic yet left out
in the weather, to fill with snow in winter
and promenade the embankment on summer nights.

Henryk Górecki at Auschwitz

It was a school outing –
they took us to Auschwitz.
Walking the rail track
we boys didn't dare
place our feet on the paths
shingled with human bones.

What was their reasoning –
bringing us by bus from our grey suburb?
I cannot shake it off.

Some of the boys skipped on the tracks,
calling to one another, their names
like bells in the heavy air.

When the music came to me
it was from words scrawled
on a cell wall: *Oh Mamma do not cry* –

a soaring that built and built,
but silent. My eardrums almost burst
before I laid down the first note.

Then, a single tone repeating,
became sorrow in all its forms,
that if you closed your eyes
you could smell it
and never lose that smell.

Letters to Malta

for Vikki

I. CHILD

The oak has been quiet since you left.
Almost May, and the woods are only just
beginning with their stipple of leaf.

It will be summer before the threshing
starts in the oak; the creak
and cranking of timber that netted

your hands to your ears: *I'm the only one
that sleeps at the back*, you'd say,
if lightning strikes, if it falls, which way?

The wind that disturbs our oak is that
same wind that brought you home from school
with all the seasons in your hair,

aromas scenting your silkiness
with summer grass and autumn fires,
frost blooming your skin to a russet apple.

There are beautiful words for winds,
the world is smaller for that:
Boreas, mistral, sirocco, simoom,

recite them child –
trade them back on the wind.

II. DAUGHTER

It's here, you say,
sixty miles south of Sicily,
a footprint north of the Libyan desert,
in flying time not far.

The airport is pushy with pensioners
off to their winter sun,
disapproving of youth
with excess baggage –
the keepsakes and necessities
that vied for space; layers
of clothing that still don't
hide your slender frame.

Last hugs and kisses
before you move to Departures.
No looking back
but a turn to your partner –
a look that quivers with questions.

Then, as in the Soaps,
when somebody says, *come with me*
and two characters disappear,
the smoked glass doors
of Passport Control conceal you.

Back at the house
the map on the floor:
MALTA. The word
bigger than its boundaries,
an island smaller than my little fingernail,
surrounded by sea and sea and sea.

III. WOMAN

Loss hangs about your room
where the curtains stay open
and night looks in
with its dark stare.
It paces the tidy bed,
uncluttered tops of furniture.

But here you are rescued,
here, in these dried grasses
filling a straight glass vase;
in the painted pottery jugs
carefully placed on a pine shelf.

Your home is somewhere out at sea,
and each visit sees you trailing
cargo in accurate weights
over non-foetal waters.

You're 'the English girl' now,
hanging washing on a roof,
learning to live with the harsh sun.
At night, when you watch it sink,
turning tiered rocks to rose,
you might sometimes hear me call
I miss you –

Or as you run to the terrace
to watch fireworks and catch
the glint of the moon, you recall
how it bloomed in the trees
at the back of the house
then flooded into your room.

IV. ANGEL

You would be the first to admit
you've never been an angel. But after
our first visit, when the photographs
had been developed – there you were –
in the courtyard of the Grand Masters' Palace,
standing under a stone eagle,
its long neck and beak crowning
your head, its large wings
perfectly placed and symmetrical,
mysteriously giving you properties of flight,
even in wings of stone.

V. POSTCARD FROM ASSISI, 1998

The cracks are large, craters pull
the dove-soft stone apart.

Go and repair my house –
this is what the crucifix whispered to St. Francis.

I enter his church,
the frescoes drift around me,
I am encompassed in clear blues, the palest of pinks.

(Remember our little earthquake in England –
you woke and felt your bed shake,
only you in the house felt it.)

I stand in the Basilica
as people swarm around me,
a tremor moves through my whole body.

The loss I feel is not imaginary –
even Art is mortal;
could return to dust.

VI. BALCONY

You know how a woman in Valletta will lean
from her balcony and call across streets
to another woman, and although she cannot see
the person she is calling, she hears answer
and is satisfied,
that is how I call to you now.

VII. EX-PAT

You are returning –
                migrating from the South;

Trading Mediterranean life
                for an English autumn;

A bird pulled on thermals
                of belonging;

Leaving warm southerlies,
                the violence of a mistral,

To live again
           in a temperate climate,

Where falling leaves
               clog railway lines,

A night of snow
               halts progress on roads.

The pull inside the cage of your chest
                              takes you soaring –

Above clouds like snow drifts,
               until the sea changes colour

And the greens and the greys
               are the ones you were born to;

Leaping back in your flesh,
               as you descend in the thrilling air.

Winter Coats

It was that day when one season
changes to another – when Venetians
hang their winter coats on high
lines above narrow courtyards
between their tall houses.

And we were lying in a hotel bedroom,
on a bed, where the coats – mainly furs –
hung outside our open window, sending
in a warm breeze and slanting sun
to tantalize our naked flesh.

As we turned on the bed, the chandelier
on the high ceiling caught the light
and dripped patterns on your arms,
as though your skin was the lagoon,
dappled by evening sun.

Then, even in the heat of Venice,
where the only sound was water
from the fountain in a nearby square,
one strong memory came back to me:

the coldest night of winter in England,
when you piled the frozen bed high
with all the blankets you could find,
and your long winter coat,
to make us a cave.

The Open Window

after Pierre Bonnard

As dusk fell
I kept the window open,
the shutters pushed right back,
watched everything changing
as the sky gloomed over the trees,
mixing its dense blue
with shimmering purple and green;
the sky floating into the room, deepening
the red of the walls, as though
the breezeless night
enveloped my lethargy.

Yet there were still two elements –
the outside aloof in its grandness,
the open window no more
than an impossible invitation.
I wait for the white planet to dip
into view, feel its power
to hypnotise –
even if I pull down the sheer
black blind and fall asleep.

Memory

after René Magritte

The woman is thinking –
she places her head on the windowsill.
Her dreamhead is full of sea and clouds;
memory, a stain creeping through her brain.

How often she has been at this window,
the sea tossing her its stories,
clouds shifting their vague promises.
Today the wind brought in a leaf,

a leaf so iridescent in its youthfulness,
memory oozed like blood down her cheek.
She coils and plaits her hair,
turns love round in her hands;
stows away the present with the past.

Nothing can be forgotten:
a cinema of dreams brushes her sleeping eyes,
the future relies on this remembering.
One morning she may wake
and the whole of a wordhoard die on her lips.

Eve

After he had created Adam
there was much discussion

on, *What is Art? What is Beauty?*
I evolved in his mature period,

from a material more lasting;
the ivory of a rib could be honed,

shaped into something profound.
Maybe it was a dreamtime,

but I was aware of sounds,
as through a screen, saw

dust swirling, rising snake-like,
particles moving towards each other,

the form fell to the ground,
the wind died, Adam slept.

Next I heard argument, the whole
cosmos seemed involved:

tools thrown – everything in turmoil.
I saw an artist angry with himself.

I watched him destroy part of his first sculpture –
pull out a shining white bone.

When he began again it was like a melody
of love played over and over.

And I, who had never lain
beneath a mother's heartbeat,

would be forever in quest
for the taste of this fruit.

Penelope

I didn't recognise him –
an old man, hunched and weary
ambling up to the courtyard.
The dogs were almost on him
when someone saw
and called them off.

I think he expected me to fall
into his arms, but there
had to be some talking
and sly looking.
He was different –
I was different.

He touched my face,
I pulled away.
He stank.
It wasn't just the sea;
the salty years
ingrained in his skin,
there were other things.
I didn't want to know.

He began the story of our bed,
fashioned around the olive tree.
Such a craftsman with his voice.
Half-way through, we took
each other's hands,
and lay in it.

Bride

My mother has brought home red silk,
embroidered with birds and flowers.
Today the seamstress will call
to take my measurements.

Ibra looks kind in the photograph,
his family has been measured against mine.
The marriage will be stitched together
by our elders and ancestors.

I am having my hands decorated in readiness,
the henna is earth-coloured and will fade to straw.
My bridegroom is made of straw –
I cannot perceive him as flesh and blood.

When I make my secret visit,
the doctor takes needle and thread –
invisibly stitches a hymen:

I think of birds and flowers,
my red silk dress,
my virgin journey
to Pakistan.

Fossil

It's in the genes, they'd say,
when into your fifties you were still radiant.
We would blame them too for the invisible disease –
the arthritis you said might skip a generation.

In the end, of course, signs
were visible; palpable
in bent fingers, in grooves
of pain tracing your face.

Your hair now falls straight like silk
around your head, a faint outline
of the fossil you are becoming
on the rock face of the bed.

And fossils are such tactile things,
we have to pick them up,
read them for their history;
their place in the universe.

Somewhere in the curve of you
are genes that gave you blue-eyed
dark-haired beauty,
revealed through touch.

Flood

Flood water takes the willows
by their necks, filling the throat
of the bridge; silent beast
moving under sunlit clouds,
smooth racing pelt, pocked by the wind.

She rises to her feet – the invalid,
smelling the air of change.
Feet that cannot walk,
with new cunning
move to a window.

The day is drowning,
water meadows drowned,
sun is water in the shining,
willows frantic on the islands.

And in the lowering twilight,
her compulsory bed
rocking away on the current.

Inheritance

I brought you Spring but you were dying.
How many deaths have I endured since,
knowing I could not return to lose
you again and again? The daffodils
abandoned on the bed would wilt –
there was no vase for water,
and you would die with no one by your side.
How cold your first-born daughter.

Equal to the seed, your mystery
charged my head with words;
photographs with Arabs in the desert,
the lands of war you never spoke of.
Then the forests of North Wales I grew to know –
the pungent smell, the crackle underfoot.
These things crept into my senses like daybreak,
silently, irreversibly, became my inscape.

The Brink

i.m. Andrew, July 1978 – April 2005

Before I go over your death again,
I will think of some poets I love
and how their deaths were tragic.

How Edward Thomas was killed
in the last moment of war,
clinging to a world where
nature was his salve.

Or Sylvia Plath, whose art
flashed through her life
like sunlight catching a mirror,
multiplied by the mirror's broken facets;

and how Keats, whose short life,
lamented by many, turned
the munificence of the world
into a throbbing heart.

I am thinking now of the nuthatch
that flew into our window this summer
and lay passive outside our door,
its neck broken –

the colours of its beauty
still pulsing somewhere
in this imperilled world.

Giverny

It's the blue that enchants –
from huge irises bordering the path
to Japanese prints on sky-blue walls.
Even the tablecloth, embroidered
with iris, faded to shadows,
fills your eyes with blue.
You look down from the bridge
on the pond floating with lily pads
and realise he stood there too,
his eyes screened with cataracts,
making the colours merge and blur.
I would like to paint as a bird sings,
he said, and you feel
in this infinite world of water
where willows dip into shadowed green
that sublime sense of a bird,
singing the colours of his dream.

Heron

You dip your fingers
as the heron picks
silently in the shallow brook.

Slow beady eyes,
slinky as the grey
reflected stones.

In a nave of trees
you keep a cathedral aura,
cool as its dank walls;

but resonant with notes,
reedy as organ pipes
that quiver in your finger ends.

Pianist or heron, I know not which.
I shall watch you as I
secretly watch the heron.

Bare trees

Through the windows of the gallery
the huge trees want to step in;
become part of the leaf-mosaic walls.

The trees stand in line, intent on breaking
through the plate-glass windows to clothe
themselves in ivy wallpaper.

Do they know how choked they would be?
Not because of the words emanating from poets,
or the music from the violin and balalaika,

but because the ivy wallpaper
would strangle and smother them –
cover their strong, knuckled limbs,

suck the air that traces every branch.
Better they stay outside,
keep their roots firmly in the park,

where a couple push a pram between their trunks,
and the winter light becomes dusky,
settling into the canvas of their architecture.

Drowned

*On February 5th, 2004, twenty-three Chinese
cockle pickers drowned in Morecambe Bay.*

cocklers in dark groups,
　stooped to their panniers harvest,
　　a blaze of red sky.

　　　　　wind off the current
　　　　　　plying the tide's secret paths,
　　　　　　looping the quicksands.

　　　　　　gulls dipping the surf,
　　　　　　　winging and whittling caught fish,
　　　　　　tracing the high wave.

　　sun at its vespers,
　　　tolling the great ocean's bell,
　　　　waving　　　drowning.

Laptop Lover

He takes her into *Road Chef*
she's slim, in office grey.

Between his scone and pot of tea
he lifts her face to his;

downloads her from her cloister
and mimes a little kiss.

She follows his manoeuvres,
laps up his every word,

her spelling is immaculate –
his eyes can't move from hers.

His fingers on her image
will shift and ask for help:

the contract will be sanctioned
in silence and with stealth.

Guidelines for Illuminators

from Cennino d'Andrea Cennini's
Il Libro dell 'Arte c. 15th Century

Arrange your life as though you are studying
theology or philosophy.

Eat and drink moderately,
saving and sparing your hand.

Preserve it from strain,
such as heaving crowbars or stones,

and other things –
that if indulged

can make your hand
so unsteady it will waver,

fluttering more than leaves
in the wind.

This indulgence I warn against:
the company of women.

This is Just to Say…

apologies to William Carlos Williams

I have cooked
the courgettes
that you were putting
in the vegetable show

and which you
probably thought
would win
first prize.

Forgive me –
they were all we had
to feed
my vegetarian lover.

Falling for Milton

In the class on Milton's *Paradise Lost*,
a woman peels and eats an apple;
asks the unanswerable question:
what is the 'Knowledge'?

The class of fourteen Eves
and half-a-dozen Adams
debate the devil's strategy (Book Two),
enlightenment must wait.

Her appetite replete,
and showing no apparent sexuality,
she wraps her peel in tissue,
pulls down her woolly hat.

The Taxidermist

They are magnificent in their
immobile state; a landscaped window
showing them to perfection.

I passed them every day
on my way to school, until
the unnatural became ordinary.

The barn owl, its huge expanse
of white wings, gazing out at me,
a stoat's bright-eyed stare –
curiosities never glimpsed in real life.

Years later I photographed the window,
saw pike, static inside a tank,
only yards from the river,
owls peering through glass,
poised to fly to the hooting woods.

I think about the taxidermist, skinning,
preserving, mounting on armature,
trophies to adorn country estates,
and question why I loved that
window so much, how it stayed
in my memory, as though
I was under a spell.

Escape Artist

She will never forget it –
the glass box of the near-drowning,
water churning in panic, plummeting
twice to the riverbed,
until suddenly, silence, tranquillity;
a world like a lantern show
and her life falling backwards in images.

Sometimes the memory rises –
still anchored in that part of the river,
like a part of her is still in it;
water reeds feathering its walls,
fish circling, eyes wide open,
descants of bubbles pouring
from pouting mouths.

Disappearing Men

Thoreau disappeared into the woods for months,
whereas Frost always wanted to.
How deep those woods –
what refuge from life.
And how men crave with
a passion a Houdini spell.

Some disappear forever
from wives, from children,
thinking they can start anew;
here they are –
on the train under caps,
tuning in, shutting out life,
dreaming in their earphones
the music of the woods.

Luggage

When he left
he took her favourite dress;
sneaked it into a holdall

imagined her looking for it,
her irritation as she flicked
through her wardrobe.

Saw her bewilderment,
her blue eyes staring
into the past –

the last time she wore it –
that night she felt
his fingers on her spine,

her neck, through her hair,
the dress forcing her
to think of him

instead of leaving him stranded
in a room with a holdall –
a red dress hanging on the door.

Desert Ghosts

There is no fear of attack –
these are the silent movers,
lifting with the heat haze
in the no-man's land
between tank and village.

Not part of the desert
but of the desert winds,
the mind of the desert,
the mind of the half-sleeping soldier;
filmic shadows that cannot attack.

Each night in dreams
they rise under moonlight,
soft robes flowing, turbans unwinding –
tinsmith, blacksmith, goatherd and nomad,
in an alchemy of sand and dust.

From the scarred no-man's land
between the tanks and the village,
these ghosts of the desert
enter the soldier's mind.

Boy Singer

In my dream
we were dancing –
the landscape moved,
rotating its sails,
borders fogged.

When the Taliban came
we buried the instruments
beneath the floors,
but on nights like this
we heard them,
taut strings shivering
as we whirled,
wild as flurries of snow.

I was the boy
with the beautiful voice
who sang at weddings;
songs of longing;
hypnotic laments
to hold the sky still.

But in this dream
our souls were buried
deep in the ground –
the *tanbour* calling.

Over the Border

When I wake I will find
Russia hauled up in front of me,
its pure white light
streaming from morning
down the remembered avenues

out of Pushkin and Gorky,
Pasternak's snow-filled rivers,
Brodsky's Neva and the lines
of women waiting that Akhmatova
still haunts your heart with.

Nearing Petersburg, the *dachas*
under trees, dilapidated
as the women who pad
in slippers and headscarves,
until the grey apartments, block

on block, blank each other
in curtainless blandness:
our comfortable hotel, facing
Baltic waves like tidal stone,
lashing the concrete shore,

where the floor moved
on its watery foundations –
a kind of lurching for a split second,
as if in preparation
for the shock of the sublime;

when you see the floating palaces
lining the Neva's embankments,
trembling on the unpredictability
of water and history.

The Asphalt Road

She takes off – cruises the asphalt –
long straight roads that lead to Chernobyl.

In this somnambulant world, mushrooms,
wild-flowers, wolves and boars
follow some instinct to thrive;
grass grows through the bonnets of tractors,
washing still hangs in the backs of houses.

On windowsills, photographs fade
in thick grey dust, among
medicine bottles and dolls
with blackened skin.

The asphalt road is the safe place –
repels radiation. She opens the throttle,
speeds on past the forest
where trees had glowed red.

The ghost towns draw her –
their roads to nowhere.
She takes more photographs,
then leaves this landscape
where nature pushes abundance
on a place where the clocks have stopped.

That Afternoon

That's how it seemed that afternoon –
dust flying, clogging the sun.
They were clearing their homes –
little things, a doll, a photo,
hands moving fast – minds faster.

Reporters would follow –
catch some child ragged, solitary,
staring right into the lens for them;
huge eyes, dirt tracks down her cheeks
where tears had been;

would never fall again.
The whole sun that afternoon
seemed dust-ridden, useless.
The country a dust-ball
rolling.

Sweet Idleness

after 'Dolce Far Niente'
by John William Godward 1861 – 1922

Oh yes, of course, my goddess wears these well.
I brought her many riches, truth to tell,
when visiting the Orient. That marble pool
she languishes beside was shipped to Liverpool
from best Italian mines. She dips her hands,
then lies and dreams on skins from lands
she'll only hear about when great men talk –
boast about adventures when they stalked
out animals for ivory and furs.

That passion! She's almost like a cat that purrs,
and in her idleness she must be glad
to know a man like me. I've had
the spoils of wealth. She's one. The painter's art
can only show what's there: munificence of my heart.

Nude in Movement

after Marc Chagall

When he said, *Take off your clothes and spread your legs,
bend your head to cover one breast*, I didn't think too much.
After all, he's painted me in many strange positions and places:
up in the sky like a parachute, riding the back of a rooster.

Look here, I said, *are you sure about this? I mean, it's not just
uncomfortable, but who wants to see me cracks and all?
I can't hold this pose for long.* Now it's wicked the thing
he's gone and done, we only fell out for a day but I'm plastered
all over the net, in shameless revealing contortions.

Even now, when he's had his revenge, he's still got his head
in that cloud, dreaming a masterpiece, as I cover myself
from head to toe and dodge the paparazzi.

Vincent

Named after a dead brother,
how you struggled to find
identity. Those drawings of
peasants in Belgium;
the miners, whose darkness you felt.

Your story haunts me –
always moving further South –
the yellow house in Provence,
the letters to Theo,
that calligraphy of your
name on each painting.

The only impulse was to
paint what you woke to, and felt,
in the skies and wheat fields of the South.
Paintings where the greens and yellows
boiled with emotion and the mistral
caught with the seizures in your head.

The asylum kept you
away from the landscape,
but you painted the garden
through your window. Then Theo's
child was born and another seizure.
You smeared your face with coal dust,
asked Theo to rescue you.

But the South had done for you,
and in Auvers you moved nearer
to your only conclusion: a gun
in the side – for Theo's family –
their baby named Vincent after you.

'Window of Vincent's Studio at the Asylum, 1889'

From the outside it looked menacing –
a grilled window, beautifully arched.
I knew you looked out on the garden from there,
watched other inmates circling,
heads bent. But now

I see the inside in your painting –
and how you could always adapt
your circumstances to fire your art:
boxes of paint piled up, drawings
on the walls. Walls you must have painted –
as ochre as Roussillon.

The pain of your illness was excruciating,
but the window looked out on blue sky,
spring-woken leaves, enticing you back to health,
confirming the power in nature you drew on,
injecting it like a drug.

Moon Walk – July 1969

for Dawn

The hospital silent at night,
padding the corridors, heavy with milk,
I watch white, swirling images on the screen.

Men walking on the moon!
And you born into this new world.
Tiny fingers curl around mine,

your body still holding its foetus shape,
as moving through vaporous moonscape
men step into the unknown.

This ward, this night flowing with exploration.
Beginnings. Love coming into being –
as you open your eyes and we look

at each other. Inside those pools,
depths never charted before,
newer than space discovery,

newer than infinite astronomy.

Acknowledgements

A number of poems from the collection have previously been published. Thanks go to the editors of the following magazines, journals and anthologies:

Acumen, Equinox, The Interpreter's House, Magma, New Welsh Review, Orbis, Poetry Nottingham, Poetry Review, Envoi, The Frogmore Papers, The Dawntreader and *Sarasvati* (Indigo Dreams), *Poetry Wales, Quattrocentto, Scintilla, Seam, Seventh Quarry, Staple, The North, The High Window Journal,* The Cheshire Prize anthologies 2004, 2007, and 2010. Best of Manchester Poets 2011, Sandburg Livesay Award 1999, Welsh Women's Poetry 1460–2001, (Honno Classics).

I would also like to acknowledge *Making Faces* by John Prag and Richard Neave for details of the re-construction of *The Yde Girl*.

Notes on the poems

Arno
The river Arno runs through Florence, Italy.

The Yde girl
Discovered in 1897 near the northern Dutch town of Assen, the Yde Girl was dated to the first centuries BC/AD. A waxwork reconstruction was undertaken in 1992, now in the museum in Drenthe.

The Bones Dreaming
In Northern Italy, February 2007, archaeologists discovered the skeletons of a couple locked in an embrace. The burial dates to the Neolithic period (5000–4000 BC).

In the Footsteps of Bashō
Bashō, 17th century poet of Haiku, whose perilous journeys through Japan capture the transience of the natural world.

Iron Shoes on the Embankment
'Shoes on the Danube Bank' in Budapest is a memorial to the Jews shot into the river in 1945 during the time of the Arrow Cross terror.

Henryk Górecki at Auschwitz
'Symphony of Sorrowful Songs' was composed in 1976. In 1992 it topped the classical charts in Britain and the United States.

Giverny
Monet's house in Normandy.

Boy Singer
Tanbour – a long-necked string instrument.

Over the Border

Pushkin – Alexander Pushkin, 1799–1837, Russian poet, novelist, dramatist, and short-story writer.

Gorky – Maxim Gorky, also spelled Maksim Gorky, pseudonym of Aleksey Maksimovich Peshkov, 1868–1936, Russian short-story writer and novelist.

Pasternak – Boris Leonidovich Pasternak, 1890–1960. Russian poet, novelist, and literary translator.

Brodsky – Iosif (Joseph) Aleksandrovich Brodsky, 1940–1996. Russian and American poet and essayist.

Akhmatova – Anna Akhmatova, pseudonym of Anna Andreyevna Gorenko, 1889–1966. Russian poet.

Dachas – Russian; a summer residence or cottage.